30 DAYS TO CHANGE

GOING FROM A WHAT TO A WONDER

NICKY E. COLLINS

30 Days to Change
Copyright © 2014 Nicky E. Collins

All Rights Reserved.

Published 2014.

No part of this publication may be reproduced, distributed, or transmitted in any form or by any means, including photocopying, recording, or other electronic or mechanical methods, without the prior written permission of the publisher, except in the case of brief quotations embodied in critical reviews and certain other noncommercial uses permitted by copyright law. For permission requests, write to the publisher, addressed "Attention: Permissions Coordinator," at the address below.

First published by Faith Books & MORE

ISBN 978-1-939761-28-6

Printed in the United States of America
This book is printed on acid-free paper.

3255 Lawrenceville-Suwanee Rd.
Suite P250
Suwanee, GA 30024
publishing@faithbooksandmore.com
faithbooksandmore.com

Ordering Information:
Quantity sales. Special discounts are available on quantity purchases by corporations, associations, and others. For details, contact the publisher at the address above.

Orders by U.S. trade bookstores and wholesalers. Please contact Ingram Book Company: Tel: (800) 937-8000;
Email: orders@ingrambook.com or visit ipage.ingrambook.com.

DEDICATION

This book is dedicated to the people everywhere who truly want change to happen in their lives!
~It Will Come To Pass

FOREWORD

The Bible says in Proverbs 31:30 that a woman who fears the Lord is worthy to be praised. I knew from the first time I met my wife, that she had a reverence for God...His Word...and The Call on her Life beyond what words can even describe. She was a one of a kind woman with a special anointing to free people from obstacles that have been holding them back. Particularly in My Life….the Word she spoke to me about how to live "Life In The Now" changed me forever. I realized that in order to move forward, I had to cherish my "Now" and see it as an opportunity to do something greater than what had been done before. I have been one of the first partakers of the 30-days of wisdom she shares in this book about how to truly change your Life. She often tells me, "Change isn't Change until it's Changed!" I'm telling you this book is a wonderful roadmap to help you see real change happen in your Life, once and for all.

Pastor Carlos L. Collins
Higher Dimension Church Tallahassee
"Where The People Are Great"

DISCLAIMER

The purpose of this book is to empower, educate, and offer hope. The authors of the book achieved that through their own experiences, expertise, and research. Consequently, this book should only be used as a road map. This book is not intended to be nor is it represented as legal advice. The authors are not liable or responsible, to any person, or entity, for any and all claims, demands, damages, causes of action, suits in equity of whatever kind or nature, caused or alleged to have been caused, directly or indirectly, by the information contained in this book or the authors' past or future negligence or wrongful acts.

INTRODUCTION

My Life Has Changed. It didn't happen overnight, but it happened moment by moment. God took what I thought was nothing and turned it into something, as I surrendered my thoughts, my vision and all of my plans to Him.
Our Motto is: Purpose Over Everything!

Today, I no longer give in to my own fears, insecurities, doubts and unbelief about what God has called me to do/become. I know first hand that one act of obedience to what God is saying, can and will change your Life forever. As you read the next pages, join me in making up your mind to do what God is asking you to do, no more excuses. This is our time to change, and see God show up in our lives like never before. I am a living witness that God can take you from being "A What"...the point in your Life when people totally misunderstand you, to "A Wonder"...when your Life becomes so astonishing and inspiring that it leaves people in awe. Now Is Your Time!

"We never grow closer to God when we just live life. It takes deliberate pursuit and attentiveness."
-Francis Chan

RECEIVE YOUR CHANGE

You have to recognize and admit that you need to change before you can receive your change! Salvation and repentance is first! Trust me, I tried to change on my own, but it didn't work! I ran from church to church, person to person, thinking that would change me, but it didn't. My true and lasting change only happened when I gave my Life to Jesus Christ. You need God...You need the Lord...You need Help. You also need people around you who have your best interest...who can hold you accountable. Relationships are so important... healthy relationships. Make up your mind to receive change, once and for all!

Today

Evaluate Your Relationships
God...Family...Friends
(How can these relationships improve?)

"Your greatest Blessing is on the other side of your obedience!"
-Nicky E. Collins

IT TAKES COMMITMENT

There was a time in my Life that I couldn't commit to anything. Fear would rise up...and prevent my ability to commit. The only thing you can receive is what you're committed to. Vision can't come to pass without a root...and the root feeds the Vision. If you have no root...you have no Vision, so you can't grow and last. When I knew there was a call on my Life and truly became focused on that, even through the most trying situations...I stayed committed to God. We have to know commitment is not just what we say, it's what we do! Commitment is about being obedient to what God is telling you to do.

Today

Commit To Do Something!
(What Are Your Next Steps?)

"The greatest mistake we can make is to stay on the ground after falling."
-Victor Manuel Riviera

YOU DON'T HAVE TO BE PERFECT

We all make mistakes. If someone tells you they haven't made any mistakes...they are not telling the truth. The key is how you see your mistake when you make it and what you do with what you learn from it. Change comes out of knowing there's a need for it. Every time you make a mistake, it shows you some area in your Life where change is needed. Don't be afraid of your imperfections...embrace them and work to get beyond them.

Today

Write down three imperfections you will pray and trust God to help you get beyond.

"Don't let your past mistakes be the foundation for you future."
-Nicky E. Collins

YOUR PAST HAS ITS BENEFITS

Your Past is a testament of who you are. Embrace it and move forward. You can't change the past...but you can change your "Now" for a better future. Make the decision, instead of letting your past hold you back, to use it as a testimony to pay you! The main key is you must make a decision to get beyond it.

Here are the steps:
Embrace It (Talk about what happened, etc.)
Make a quality decision (Not to repeat it)
Move Forward(No looking back)

Today

Identify the one thing from your past that has been holding you back. Write it down, talk it out with someone, and then write down what you will do now to get beyond it.

"This life is what you make it." -Marilyn Monroe

LIFE IS NOT ALWAYS A PARTY

You have to take the good and the bad out of Life. You have to mentally accept that you will have some bad days, but that doesn't change or have to affect your final outcome. Your attitude while you're going through determines your outcome. Stay in the place of Faith...where you're trusting that change is happening! You have to stay in an attitude of Faith no matter what!

Today

Identify one "Hot Button" issue that usually triggers negative emotions in your Life. Write it down and add it to your prayer list for God to remove it. Pray until it's no longer an issue.

"I want you to take stock of your words, because whether you realize it or not, your life is the sum total of all the words you have spoken."
-Pastor Creflo Dollar

WHO CARES WHAT "THEY" SAY

It's time to take a stand for your Life. I often tell people you're the Prophet of your own house. It's not about what people speak over your Life, it's about what you say about yourself. Changing your perspective about yourself starts by making the conscious decision to surround yourself with Truth. The Word of God will tell you the Truth about your Life. Also... be sure that you surround yourself with people who support the True You!

Today

Speak Positive over your Life for the next 24-hours.
Write a journal entry about your experience.

"Every time you ask for forgiveness, you declare that your life does not belong to you, but has been created for the purpose of Another."
-Paul David Tripp

FORGIVE THEM AND YOU

This really sounds easier than it actually is...but it's absolutely necessary. My Faith tells me God forgave us and sent His only Son...Jesus Christ to die and become a sacrifice for us to continually walk in forgiveness. Knowing this, it's very hard to walk around in unforgiveness when you've received forgiveness over and over again. I really think sometimes we believe forgiving ourselves and those who have wronged us... seems like we're not taking into account what we've done or what has happened to us. Instead, we have to see forgiveness as the part of the process that signifies we have gotten over the issue and are ready to freely move forward. No more being so judgemental towards other people. This is your time to move on and complete your process of change.

Today

Identify three people/areas in your Life where forgiveness needs to take place. What's the very next thing you'll do to work towards forgiveness?

"Have patience. All things are difficult before they become easy." -Sa'di

USE YOUR PAIN TO FUEL YOUR PURPOSE

Pain stops us from change. The only way to stop this negative cycle is to use the pain to push forward vs. falling backwards. We all have experienced hurt in some sort of way, but we must keep moving forward. When there's no forward progress... you become stagnant...and everything around you seems to be void of Life. Push Forward...at all costs, knowing that the temporary pain you feel will be worth it in the end.

Today

Identify some things in your Life that have caused pain. Now, make a decision to move Forward!

"To be healed is a choice that happens in your mind first"
-Michelle Salvant

HEALING IS A PROCESS

Don't expect for things to just happen over night. Just like with healing in your body...you have to visit the doctor, take your medication and allow healing to manifest itself in your Life. The same is true for inner healing. There's a process and you have to be willing to submit to the process to get the desired results. You must forgive, love and live again.

Today

Make This Confession…I have been forgiven…so I forgive.

"God's grace will not take you where it cannot keep you." -Edmond Sanganyado

SEEK GOD FOR INSTRUCTIONS

God will never lead you wrong. Doing it our way, always leaves room for doubt. God's instructions will always lead you to your next destination. Sometimes it will not be where you want to go...but it will be where you need to be. Follow God's lead.

Today

Ask God what is my next step?
Write down the first answer that comes to mind.

"I will prepare and some day my chance will come."
-Abraham Lincoln

ARE YOU PREPARED TO RECEIVE WHAT YOU ARE PRAYING FOR?

We pray for a lot of things...but when they come, are we really ready to receive them? Are you learning and really preparing for what it takes to handle your Blessings? The truth is, if the Blessing comes and you're not ready, it will eventually become a curse to you. Only God can truly prepare you for what He has for you. Seek Him, with pureness of heart and true motives. That's how you truly prepare for all He has for you!

Today

Write down one thing you are believing God for… and then write down some things you are doing to truly prepare for it.

"Feed Your Faith and Starve Your Doubts To Death"
-Dr. Lester Sumrall

FEED YOUR FAITH

You must keep positivity around you! You have to keep it in your eyes, ears, etc. Reading a book, speaking positive affirmations over your Life, connecting with empowering people…all of those things help keep your Faith in tact. Feeding your Faith is not an option, it's absolutely necessary in your process of receiving true change.

Today

Name at least one thing you will do for the rest of this month to Feed Your Faith.

"All of us have a place in History"
-Richard Brautigan

PURPOSE OVER EVERYTHING

When it comes to your Life...Purpose should be the priority. Purpose is simply the reason why you were created...and life is about finding it and living it. You have to know you have Purpose and you are not here by accident or coincidence. There is a divine purpose for your Life! God shall get the Glory out of your Life!

Today

Do you know your Purpose in Life?
Prayer: God, reveal to me/show me what I was created for!
In Jesus Name, Amen.

"For it is in giving that we receive." -Francis of Assisi

KEEP SOWING

The Bible says as long as the earth remains, there will be seed, time and harvest. We should never get in a position where we stop giving/stop sowing. As long as the earth remains...that's what keeps you going. Your seed keeps you vibrant. Your seed literally keeps you alive. It doesn't matter how much you've sown in the past...seed is always in the Now! Sow your time, talent, and treasure today!

Today

Purpose in your heart to give without reservation. Sow an uncommon seed into good ground.

"In life, people are doing one of two things...Inspiring you to be Better...or Expiring You!"
-Bishop Abiola Idowu

STAY ROOTED

Sometimes there's a Blessing in your stillness. Many times we get so anxious for something, we pluck up everything God has been doing under the surface. There's power in the connections you have! If your root is good, your fruit will be good. Where are you planted? Who's feeding you? Check your connections!

Today

Identify your key connections...Personally, Spiritually, Professionally. Are they inspiring or expiring you?

"The future belongs to those who believe in the beauty of their dreams."
-Eleanor Roosevelt

DON'T GIVE UP ON YOUR DREAMS

It doesn't matter what people say or do...whatever dream you have, keep striving for it. God gave you that dream, you didn't just come up with it. Keep going...Keep pressing! There's an appointed time for it to happen. The question is, will you be there when it shows up? Many times it's our dreams that fuel the life within us, because they keep us looking ahead. Keep Dreaming!

Today

Write down one dream God has given you.
Make a declaration that you will not give up on it!

"Jump or stay in the boat."
-Margaret Stohl

DECISIONS

A decision is defined as a conclusion or resolution reached after consideration. We are always going to be in a position where we will have to make decisions. The key is to count the costs and then make a choice. If you don't, you make the choice to allow whatever happens to happen. Make your own choice! Decisions are good, and when you make one, stick with it. Also, be sure to take every decision to God. He thinks on a higher level than we do!

Today

Make one decision, once and for all...that is necessary for you to move forward. Write it down with date and time, and keep moving from there!

"You can go as far as you think, imagine and dream. Anything is possible."
-Lailah Gifty Akita

EXPAND YOUR MIND

You have to think beyond what you've always thought. Open up to all options and see things from a different perspective. We must be open to the way God wants to do things in our Life. See things from a broader perspective. Many of our questions will be answered if we just look at things from another point of view. God has a million ways to Bless you.

Today

Try at least one thing new.
See something from a different perspective.

"When what you want becomes what you need, God will show up"
-Nicky E. Collins

WANTING WHAT YOU NEED

A lot of times, we want what we want. We want things that are not good for us. We want things that will appease our flesh and make us feel proud and happy. We want something we can brag on from what we see on the outside, but really it's no good for us within. God never said He would supply our wants, He said He would supply our needs. When you begin to want what you need...you will never be in lack. Just like David said, when the Lord becomes your Shepherd...when He truly becomes the priority, you will never be in lack...you will never want!

Today

Repeat this Prayer…
Lord, not my will…let your will be done. Lord, I cast all of my wants on you…and I lean and depend on you to supply my every need.

"If I must start somewhere, right here and now is the best place imaginable."
-Richelle E. Goodrich

GOD IS WAITING ON YOU

Many times we get stuck where we are, saying that we are waiting on God to speak or do something. The truth is, God is really waiting on you to do something. God is asking what did you do with the last plan I gave you? Did you finish the last assignment? God is waiting on you to put your Faith in action!

Today

What is the last thing God told you to do? Did you finish it/why or why not? What are you planning to do about it right now?

"A journey of a thousand miles begins with a single step" -Lao-tzu

OBEDIENCE TO GOD IS EVERYTHING

Please know that you don't have to understand everything God tells you to do! He may not reveal every detail to you, but when you do what He says, it will bring you into a whole new place. This is what builds your relationship with God and opens you up to trusting Him in new ways. It starts with the little things. Small acts of obedience lead to big results. When you do what God asks you to do, it Blesses people and makes God proud. That's what it means to be used by God. Today, be sensitive to His Spirit. It will set you on a whole new course for your Life.

Today

Make up your Mind that you will obey God…
No Matter What!

"Somewhere inside you is a masterpiece waiting to be exposed." -Raimy Diaz

THE REAL YOU

Get in touch with the real you! What's really holding you back? What are you waiting on to move forward. When you stop making excuses for what's going on in your Life, and deal with the reality of where you are, what you're feeling and what you're thinking...that is when you'll be able to really tap into the real you. No more covering things up so people can accept you. You can no longer do it for people, it's time to do something for yourself!

Today

Make this Confession:
I am no longer bound by people and their expectations.
I surrender to the will of God for my Life.
I will Move Forward!

"Even when you don't see Him working, He's busy working on your behalf."
-Yvonne Pierre

THE BATTLE IS WORKING FOR YOUR GOOD

We shouldn't make everything out to be a war. Certain things happen to make us more aware that it's time to go to the next level. Every thing that seems bad in our lives is not brought on by the devil. Some things are necessary for our growth. You can be confident that every battle we face, Jesus has already won. All we have to do is walk in Victory!

Today

Settle it in your Mind…
God will fight your battle…and He will win!

"If you've got nothing to dance about, find a reason to sing." -Melody Carstairs

BE HAPPY!

Every now and then...you have to will yourself to be happy. You have to think happy thoughts...think yourself into a happy place. The joy of the Lord is your strength and it is the fuel for your happiness. When you're happy and you're in a happy place...you will be contagious. Be Happy!

Today

Do at least one thing that makes you happy and post about it!

"If you have a deep desire to move forward, a way is being prepared for you." –
Bryant McGill

DEAL WITH IT

It's time to open your eyes, be sober/diligent, and deal with the situations you are facing straight on! Handle your business! As for the thing that is frustrating you, it's time for you to start frustrating it! It's time to take your authority back, and put everything in its proper place. Sickness, finances, diseases, church hurt, relationships...whatever the issue is, deal with it accordingly. Stop letting issues torture you.
Deal With It!

Today

Find a day in the next two weeks that you can take off from your job, your business, or any type of work to deal with something you've been putting off for a while.

"Favor isn't fair...but it's Favor anyway!" -Various

FAVOR OVER FEAR

Don't be afraid to walk in your Favor! Be free to let your light shine. People need to be able to see the light in you, and experience your journey. It will give them hope to move forward.

Today

Confess Favor over your Life!
Speak what you want to see come to pass in your Life.

"When you come to the edge of all that you know, you must believe one of two things: there will be ground to stand on... or you will grow wings to fly."
-O.R. Melling

I'M BACK

Sometimes you have to let people talk, let them say what they want to say...as you continue to move forward. The truth is, when you come out whatever situation you're in, your testimony will be greater than what the naysayers ever said about you! You have to know that you're unstoppable. Let your Faith rise above your fear! Declare, "I'm Back!"

Today

Take 15-minutes to meditate on how far God has brought you in the past week...month...year.
Journal your thoughts.

"Opportunity doesn't make appointments, you have to be ready when it arrives."
-Tim Fargo

CONSISTENCY IS THE KEY TO THE BREAKTHROUGH

You have to be willing to work just as hard in the middle of the process as you did at the beginning. You have to be patient and willing to walk through your process, even when it seems like it's not going to happen. You must believe in yourself, and know your dreams can't come true without you! You must be consistent...keep pushing...keep pressing...keep speaking...it shall come to pass.

Today

Find something you committed to do
and haven't done in a while.
Write it down, and do something about it.
Track your progress.

"Instead of trying to control the outcome, just enjoy the journey." -Dawn Gluskin

GO THROUGH YOUR PROCESS

All of You...None Of Me, that's the secret to truly allowing your change to take place. You have to come to a place of surrendering and letting God be God. You will start to see things happening, when you get out of the way. All of You Lord, And None of Me.

Today

Make a decision to release your agenda...and receive what God has for you!

"Maximize Your Now!"
-Nicky E. Collins

WHAT NOW?

Now that you've gone through each day in this devotional, I have one question for you...What are you going to do Now? You must understand that your Now is all you have, and you have to take action. Make the decision that you will move forward from here, no matter what! Take charge of your Now!

Today

How are you going to maximize your now?
Email Us:
info@lifeinthenow.org

ABOUT NICKY E. COLLINS

Trailblazer, Pioneer, Now Faith Ambassador, Nicky E. Collins is committed to Living by the Word of God in real time! Her Mission is simple, to empower people to maximize their "Now" and pursue their God-given destiny.

Born in Quincy, FL, Nicky received the gift of salvation at the age of 12, at St. John Church of God in Christ under the leadership of the Late Bishop E.L. Shepphard. Nearly 15 years later she rededicated her life to Christ and began serving at Neighborhood Outreach Christian Center in Quincy, FL. She was ordained on August 17, 2003 at Foundation of Faith Christian Center in Tallahassee, FL. Her ministry was later confirmed through Without Walls Intl. Ministerial Alliance in Tampa, FL.

Throughout her years of Ministry, Pastor Nicky's work has included helping to Pastor a local church, Prison ministry, Conference speaking, Authoring books, Hosting and making Television Appearances, including a special interview on TBN's Praise The Lord with Pastor Paula White.

Today, Pastor Nicky has taken her ministry gift beyond the four walls and started Life In the Now Ministries. Founded on Hebrews 11:1, the ministry is designed to encourage and equip people to pursue their purpose and fulfill their destiny Now In Christ. The ministry provides Mentoring/Life classes at Prisons, shelters, schools and other organizations through its Discovering You Project. The project teaches essential life skills to help participants "Successfully Re-enter" society and/or live productive lives. Life In The Now also provides ministry through Media...including the "Life In The Now" television broadcast and its Interactive web ministry at www.lifeinthenow.org. Nicky is a published author and has two books, including "Discovering You," which is the basis for the Discovering You Project and gives a testimony of how she overcame an ordinary life to pursue an extraordinary life in Christ

As a Minister, Speaker, Author, Wife and Mother, Nicky says the key to balancing it all is having the right foundation... Hebrews 11:1, Now Faith!

DAILY CONFESSIONS

I am The Body of Christ and Satan has no power over me. 1Corinthians 12:2

I am of God and overcome Satan. For greater is He that is in me, than he that is in the world. 1John 4:4

I will fear no evil, for Thou art with me, Lord, Your Word and Your Spirit they comfort me. Psalms 23:4

I am far from oppression, and fear does not come nigh me. Isaiah 54:14

There is no lack, for my God supplies all my needs according to His riches in glory in Christ Jesus. Philippians 4:19

The Lord has pleasure in the prosperity of His servants, and Abraham's blessings are mine. Psalms 35:27; Galatians 3:14

I trust in the Lord with all my heart, and lean not unto my own understanding. John 16:13

The Lord will perfect that which concerns me. Psalms 138:8
I am filled with the knowledge of the Lord's will in all wisdom and spiritual understanding. Colossians 1:19

I have put off the old man and have put on the new man, which is renewed in the knowledge of Him; Ephesians 1:17

I am born of God and I have world-overcoming faith residing on the inside of me. John 5:4

I will do all things through Christ which strengthens me. Philippians 4:13

The joy of the Lord is my strength. The Lord is the strength of my life. Nehemiah 8:10

I let no corrupt communication proceed out of my mouth, but that which is good for edifying, that it may minister grace to the hearer. Ephesians 4:29

I delight myself in the Lord and He gives me the desires of my heart. Psalms 37:4

I am an overcomer and I overcome by the blood of the Lamb and the word of my testimony. Revelation 12:11

The Word of God is forever settled in heaven. Therefore, I established His Word upon this Earth. Psalms 119:89

Heal me, O Lord, and I shall be healed; save Me, and I shall be saved: for thou art my praise. Jeremiah 17:14

The Lord is my Rock, and my Fortress, and my Deliverer; My God, my Strength, in whom I will trust; Psalms 18:2

Nay, in all these things I am more than a conqueror through Him that loved Me. Romans 8:37

If I abide in the Lord, and His Word abides in me, I shall ask whatever I want, and it shall be done unto me. John 15:7

ADDITIONAL BOOKS

Discovering You

Finding God's True Purpose For Your Life

The Promise Devotional...31-Days of God's Promises For Your Life

To order:
Email us at *info@lifeinthenow.org*

www.ingramcontent.com/pod-product-compliance
Lightning Source LLC
Chambersburg PA
CBHW070108100426
42743CB00012B/2692